Church Times

Living the

Exploring the Eucharist

Stephen Burns

CANTERBURY
PRESS

Norwich

First published in 2006
by the Canterbury Press Norwich
(a publishing imprint of Hymns Ancient &
Modern Limited, a registered charity)
9–17 St Alban's Place
London N1 0NX

www.scm-canterburypress.co.uk

British Library Cataloguing in Publication data

A catalogue record for this book is available
from the British Library

ISBN 1-85311-658-0/9781-85311-686-5

Typeset by Regent Typesetting, London
Printed and bound by
Gallpen Colour Print, Norwich

Contents

Introduction

Gift and Response

The Eucharist is close to the heart of faith for many of the world's Christians, described by some as faith's 'source and summit'. It is rich in meanings, and we can think of it, to begin with, as both the *gift* of Christ's self-giving – 'this is my body' – and a *response* to his command – 'do this in memory of me'. The various names given by different kinds of Christians to this central act of Christian worship themselves yield different dimensions of the meaning of the meal:

- Holy communion – the principal term used by the Anglican tradition, emphasizing unity with God and with others. 'Communion' is a deeply theological word used by Paul in relation to mealtime companionship (1 Corinthians 10.17), and also, in another context, to participation in the divine (2 Corinthians 13.13).
- Breaking of bread – a term used in some free church traditions, keeping close to the Bible by referring to an activity mentioned in Acts (Acts 2.42), and in relating a revelatory encounter with the risen Christ in the Gospel of Luke's Emmaus story (Luke 24.35).
- Mass – the principal term used by the Roman Catholic tradition; probably drawn from the Latin words of the dismissal, translated 'Go, the mass is ended'. Although the link is somewhat obscured, one good way to understand the term 'mass' is as the commissioning of worshippers to witness once they are dismissed.
- The Lord's supper – preferred by some Protestant traditions, this term emphasizes Jesus' 'institution' of the meal at the Last Supper; it also emphasizes the presidency of Christ as host.
- Eucharist – familiar in most traditions, and preferred in ecumenical

conversation, this term is drawn directly from the Greek word used in the New Testament in relation to Jesus' practice at meals (e.g. Matthew 15.36; Mark 14.27; Luke 22.17; John 6.11). It means 'thanksgiving'.

Exercise

Which term do you prefer? Why?

If these different names reveal something of the gift that is given in the Eucharist, response to Jesus' mandate to 'do this' also seems to involve endless possibilities in different times and places. Consider the liturgical scholar Gregory Dix's famous meditation:

Was ever another command so obeyed? For century after century, spreading slowly to every continent and country and among every race in earth, this action has been done, in every conceivable human circumstance, for every conceivable human need from infancy and before it to extreme old age and after it, from the pinnacles of earthly greatness to the refuge of fugitives in the caves and dens of the earth. We have found no better thing than this to do for kings at their crowning and for criminals going to the scaffold; for armies in triumph, or for a bride and bridegroom in a little country church; for the proclamation of a dogma or for a good crop of wheat; for the wisdom of the Parliament of a mighty nation or for a sick old woman afraid to die; for a schoolboy sitting an examination or for Columbus setting out to discover America; for the famine of whole provinces or for the soul of a dead lover; in thankfulness because my father did not die of pneumonia; for a village headman much tempted to return to fetish because the yams have failed; because the Turk was at the gates of Vienna; for the repentance of Margaret; for the settlement of a strike; for a son for a barren woman; for Captain so-and-so, wounded and a prisoner of war; while the lions roared in the nearby amphitheatre; on the beach at

Dunkirk; while the hiss of scythes in the thick June grass came faintly through the windows of the church; tremulously, by an old monk on the fiftieth anniversary of his vows; furtively, by an exiled bishop who had hewn timber all day in a prison camp near Murmansk; gorgeously, for the canonization of St Joan of Arc – one could fill many pages with the reasons why we have done this, and not tell a hundredth part of them. And best of all, week by week and month by month, on a hundred thousand successive Sundays, faithfully, unfailingly, across all the parishes of Christendom, the pastors have done this just to *make* the *plebs sancta Dei* – the holy common people of God.

Huck, *A Sourcebook about Liturgy*, pp. 95–6

Your church will include people who can themselves give extraordinary testimony to the diversity of situations and life-circumstances in which they have celebrated the Eucharist.

Exercise

Are those people willing to share any of their stories of what the Eucharistic celebration meant to them in different times and places?

This study guide is intended for those who may be searching or new to faith and so approaching or just beginning to participate in worship. But it is also for those who have perhaps celebrated the Eucharist for many decades, for whom the guide aims to offer new insight in particular by emphasizing some of the fundamental dynamics of *contemporary* understanding. The point of a contemporary emphasis is of course not to disparage inherited and long-held perspectives, but rather to enrich them. And, as we shall see, *contemporary* perspectives on the Eucharist are deeply rooted in *ancient* understandings and practices, drawing particularly on our knowledge of the early Church – and deliberately so, for this has the advantage of sidestepping some of the divisions that emerged in the eucharistic – and other – theologies of Christian communities in medieval, Reformation and Counter-Reformation experience. One of the marks of contemporary thinking about worship is to take seriously not only the long-standing concern of theologians with the 'real presence' of Christ at or in the Eucharist, but also to wrestle with questions about what is sometimes, frankly, the real absence of people at worship! At the very least, thinking about the Eucharist in our times needs to be connected to a sense of mission. How can celebration of the Eucharist be made more meaningful for those without long experience of the Church's ways of worship, how can holy communion be celebrated 'so attractively, so dazzlingly, that it grabs our insides' (Hovda, 'Liturgy Shaping Us in the Christian Life', p. 146)?

The rich meanings of the Eucharist, and the many ways and places in which it has been celebrated, are themselves indicators that a short study guide to the Eucharist cannot say everything that might be said on the subject. This booklet proceeds, then, by exploring three areas in turn:

- Aspects of the origins of the Eucharist, particularly its roots in scripture.
- Contemporary celebration of the Eucharist, focusing particularly on understanding the *Common Worship* resources of the Church of England.
- An approach to eucharistic spirituality: living the thanksgiving.

1

What are the Origins of the Eucharist?

'A glutton and a drunkard'

Much of Jesus' ministry was conducted over meals. The famous Gospel stories of the woman who was a sinner (Luke 7.36–50), Martha and Mary (Luke 10.38–42) and Zacchaeus (Luke 19.1–10) are just three among many examples of his ministry around tables. Jesus' teaching and parables also addressed issues about hospitality at festive meals (two forceful examples are found in Luke 14.7–14 and Luke 14.15–24). And Jesus practised the kind of hospitality that he commended in his teaching, and this attracted criticism from some of his contemporaries. The Gospels record that he became notorious for his meals, and known as a 'glutton and a drunkard'. This slur may have been a label he liked, for he uses it of himself: 'A man came eating and drinking, and they complain: "Look, a glutton and a drunkard, a friend of tax agents and sinners"' (Luke 7.34, etc.). Whatever the truth, the phrase suggests that Jesus ate with those whom others would not, and in doing so operated a different view of purity from those who opposed him.

It is clear that Jesus' mealtime practice was remarkably different from that of some of his peers, most notably the Pharisees, who saw themselves as 'set apart' and hence excluded others from their tables in order, they supposed, to retain their holiness before God by remaining undefiled by the company of people who were 'unclean'. Jesus had few, if any, such rules about the company he kept at mealtimes – at least among Jews [1] –

---

1. The Gospels suggest that Jesus acted on different attitudes to Jews and non-Jews in relation to

and it seems that his only requirement for participation was simply that 'sinners' were themselves open to both giving and receiving forgiveness, as in the prayer he taught: 'forgive us our sins, as we forgive those who sin against us' (Luke 11.4). His practice about the sharing of food was, then, relatively lax and liberal compared to many other religious people of his day, and one way of reading the stories of Jesus' feeding miracles, involving thousands of people at a time, is as testimony to the fame of the abundantly generous welcome that Jesus extended over meals.

Divine hospitality

Hospitality seems to be the key point of meals for Jesus; his own meals were marked by inclusion rather than exclusion. And he understood the hospitality he so freely extended and celebrated at table as not merely his own, but that of the God of Israel, whose promise was that on Mount Zion

> the Lord of hosts will make for all peoples a feast of rich food, a feast of well-matured wines, of rich food filled with marrow, of well-matured wines strained clear. And he will destroy on this mountain the shroud that is cast over all peoples, the sheet that is spread over all nations; he will swallow up death for ever. Then the Lord God will wipe away the tears from all faces, and the disgrace of his people he will take away from all the earth . . .
>
> Isaiah 25.6–8

This assurance, which had been particularly precious to the Hebrew people in a time of exile, informed Jesus' vision for his meals as feasts of divine dominion when the mighty mercy of God become evident. Jesus saw his hospitality at table as enacting that divine promise, of opening up that occasion on which 'many shall come from east and west, from north

---

mealtime hospitality (see Mark 7.24–30; Matthew 15.21–8), although later, members of the early Church seemed to collapse the distinction that Jesus upheld (see, in particular, Acts 10).

and south, and will eat in the dominion of God' (Luke 13.29, etc.). His meals were absolutely integral to his conviction of the radiant invitation of God's reign.

Arguments about sacrifice

Jesus' approach of purity also related to his understanding of the temple. He viewed the commercialism in operation in the temple of his day as problematic, and like other rabbis of his time, was troubled by some of the ritual gestures that were employed in the offerings of the people's gifts. More specifically, he seems to have been concerned about the lack of people's involvement in the ritual gestures of sacrifice. For it had become possible to buy animals for sacrifice in the temple courts, and, after purchase, for these to be taken directly to the priests for ceremonial slaughter. What was lost in such an arrangement was the worshipper's gesture of offering of their own property and goods, of offering of themselves. Sacrifice had effectively become a financial transaction and, crucially in Jesus' view, the ritual gesture of laying on of one's hands on the things to be sacrificed – signifying that it was one's own, representing in a sense one's self – was diminished to the point of being lost altogether. The Gospel traditions of Jesus driving out the traders in the temple are memories of Jesus' unease with the practice of sacrifice, and indicate his concern to see in place of its present reality a 'house of prayer' (Luke 19.46, etc.) in which people could offer 'pure' sacrifices, that which authentically belonged to them and was their own.

The so-called Last Supper is to be understood in this context. Given his disappointment with the temple, Jesus began to relocate his own and his disciples' practice of sacrifice, replacing the temple with a simple table, substituting the sacrificial animal with elements of a basic meal. For Jesus, laying hands on bread around a domestic table could better represent 'my body' – the sacrifice of one's own goods and, hence, one's self to God – than the purchase of animals in the temple to be used by priests in rituals from which the people themselves were excluded. As

Bruce Chilton summarizes, 'At least bread and wine were Israel's own . . . [and i]n essence, Jesus made his meals into a rival altar' (Chilton, *Jesus' Prayer and Jesus' Eucharist*, p. 73).

The injection of new meaning into mealtimes in the period after Jesus' public argument with the temple authorities brought fresh vigour to his table companionship. Even more so than before, meals became the context of encounter with the divine, tables the place of access to God's reign. It is, then, significant that in the post-resurrection narratives of the Gospels, meals feature prominently (Luke 24.29–35, 41–3, etc.) just as they had done in the telling of the earlier public ministry of Jesus. Meals continued to open up access to the divine dominion and mediate the continued influence of Jesus in the disciples' midst.

Key witnesses in the early Church

The resurrection story situated in Emmaus offers an especially strong clue to how the Eucharist came, over time, to be celebrated in the early Church. For the story proposes two particularly powerful means of experiencing Jesus' influence: his opening of the scriptures to explain about himself (Luke 24.27, 32), and his self-disclosure to them at the breaking of the bread (Luke 24.35). In various New Testament descriptions of life in the early Church, these two features – word and meal – are practised by the early Christians (Acts 2.42; 20.7, etc.). They seem to reveal the central marks of early Christian worship. However, it is also evident that there were diverse interpretations and emphases in understanding of word and table, even within the New Testament itself (see Chilton, *Jesus' Prayer and Jesus' Eucharist*, esp. p. 93), and a fluidity of meanings certainly characterizes developments in the early Church.

Didache – outside the New Testament, the first available account of the Eucharist is that provided by the *Didache*, an early document that remained undiscovered until the late nineteenth century. It is not entirely clear from quite when it dates, but educated guesses range from between mid-first to mid-second century. It provides us with fragments of an early prayer at table:

> First, concerning the cup: We give thanks to you, our Father, for the holy vine of David your child, which you made known to us through Jesus your child. To you be glory for ever.
>
> And concerning the broken bread: We give thanks to you, our Father, for the life and knowledge which you made known to us through Jesus your child. To you be glory for ever.
>
> *Didache* 9.2–3

The *Didache* names the meal at which such thanks are given 'eucharist', insists that only the baptized may partake in it, and suggests that the sharing of bread and cup involved prayer of both praise and intercession. In a notable image that echoes Jesus' own desire that the reign of God would embrace people from the four corners of the earth, so the *Didache* asks that as grain once scattered in the fields and the grapes once dispersed over hillsides are reunited on the table in bread and wine, so the faithful would be gathered into the peace of God's dominion (*Didache* 9.3).

Among other notable features of the *Didache*, the shape and tone of the prayer over bread and wine are decidedly Jewish: the prayers resemble Jewish graces after meals. It praises Christ as God's 'child', a designation that did not become central to later doctrinal definition of Christ, which therefore seems to point to its early status. And it makes no particular reference to the cross as a lens through which the meal might be interpreted.

Apostolic Tradition – clues to the evolution of the Eucharist are few and fragmentary over the next century or so, although it is clear that there were developments in the meanings ascribed to the eucharistic gathering, notably the alignment of the language of body and blood with the memory of the cross of Jesus, so that Jesus' own emphasis on participants' offering of themselves was increasingly overwhelmed by reflection on Jesus' own attitude of self-giving in his death. Something of this emphasis can be seen in a prayer from around 215 AD, associated with, and for a long time (but no longer) believed to have come from the hand of Hippolytus. In this prayer, we find a major focus on Christ, a particular emphasis on the significance of his suffering, and we have the first available full text of eucharistic prayer:

The Lord be with you.
And with your spirit.
Up with your hearts.
We have (them) with the Lord.
Let us give thanks to the Lord.
It is fitting and right.

We render thanks to you, O God, through your beloved child Jesus Christ, whom in the last times you sent to us a savior and redeemer and angel of your will; who is your inseparable Word, through whom you made all things, and in whom you were well pleased. You sent him from heaven into a virgin's womb; and conceived in the womb, he was made flesh and was manifested as your Son, being born of the Holy Spirit and the Virgin. Fulfilling your will and gaining for you a holy people, he stretched out his hands when he should suffer, that he might release from suffering those who have believed in you.

And when he was betrayed to voluntary suffering that he might destroy death, and break the bonds of the devil, and tread down hell, and shine upon the righteous, and fix a term, and manifest the resurrection, he took bread and gave thanks to you, saying, 'Take, eat; this is my body, which shall be given for you.' Likewise also the cup, saying, 'This is my blood, which is shed for you; when you do this, you make my remembrance.'

Remembering therefore his death and resurrection, we offer to you the bread and the cup, giving you thanks because you have held us worthy to stand before you and minister to you. And we ask that you would send your Holy Spirit upon the offering of your holy Church; that, gathering her into one, you would grant to all who receive the holy things (to receive) for the fullness of the Holy Spirit for the strengthening of faith in trust; that we may praise and glorify you through your child Jesus Christ; through whom be glory and honor to you, to the Father and the Son, with the Holy Spirit, in your holy Church, both now and to the ages of ages. Amen.

Jasper and Cuming, *Prayers of the Eucharist*, pp. 34–5

Exercise

Do you recognize this text? It defines the shape of many contemporary eucharistic prayers. See what parallels you can find between it and the eucharistic liturgy used in your church.

Of undoubted importance as the first available text of eucharistic prayer, there is much that yet remains opaque about it, and some of the problems are accentuated when the prayer is taken out of the wider, though fragmentary context in which we find it in the *Apostolic Tradition*. It belongs there in a description of a consecration of a bishop, so it is not clear whether this prayer might have been used only on this particular kind of occasion or also on many others. In its wider context, it is clear that other things – such as milk and honey – were consecrated alongside bread and wine. And the instructions that relate to the prayer also clearly allow for extemporization rather than requiring that the text is used word for word: words 'of similar effect' would also suffice. Nevertheless, this particular text has taken on immense significance in recent liturgical renewal, and has become a prayer that many churches now share in common, finding a place in countless contemporary prayer books.

Justin Martyr's Apology is a document of equal if not greater importance in recent liturgical renewal. Dating from 150 AD (so earlier than

'Hippolytus'), it describes in detail a Sunday morning in a church in Rome. Eucharist is clearly part of the proceedings, as is generous attention to Hebrew scripture and to storytelling about Jesus and to documents circulating among the churches. The description given by Justin Martyr is:

> On the day named after the sun all, whether they live in the city or the countryside, are gathered together in unity. Then the records of the apostles or the writings of the prophets are read for as long as there is time. When the reader has concluded, the presider in a discourse admonishes and invites us into the pattern of these good things. Then we all stand together and offer prayer. And, as we said before, when we have concluded the prayer, bread is set out to eat, together with wine and water. The presider likewise offers up prayer and thanksgiving, as much as he can, and the people sing out their assent saying the amen. There is a distribution of the things over which thanks have been said and each person participates, and these things are sent by the deacons to those who are not present. Those who are prosperous and who desire to do so, give what they wish, according to each one's own choice, and the collection is deposited with the presider. He aids orphans and widows, those who are in want through disease or through another cause, those who are in prison, and foreigners who are sojourning here. In short, the presider is a guardian to all those who are in need . . .
>
> Lathrop, *Holy Things*, pp. 31–2

Exercise

Relate Justin's description to your last Sunday morning in church. Did the order of events unfold in similar fashion?

2

What are the Main Marks of Contemporary Celebration of the Eucharist?

The 'deep structure' of the liturgy

Justin's description has proved to be of inestimable importance to contemporary liturgical renewal in providing us with what is sometimes called 'the deep structure of the liturgy', the basic movement from one thing to the next as celebration of the Eucharist unfolds. If we consider the work of the World Council of Churches to define 'the Fundamental Pattern (*Ordo*) of the Eucharistic Service' we find that the basic outline maps directly onto Justin's description:

GATHERING of the assembly into the grace, love and koinonia of the triune God

WORD-SERVICE
Reading of the scriptures of the Old and New Testaments
Proclaiming Jesus Christ crucified and risen as the ground of our hope
(and confessing and singing our faith)
and so *interceding* for all in need and for unity
(sharing the peace to seal our prayers and prepare for the table)

TABLE-SERVICE
Giving thanks over bread and cup

Eating and drinking the holy gifts of Christ's presence
(collecting for all in need)
and so

BEING SENT (DISMISSAL) in mission in the world.

Best and Heller, *Eucharistic Worship in Ecumenical Contexts*, p. 35

This ecumenical framework breaks Justin's description down into a basic four-fold pattern: gathering, word, table, sending. Learning the pattern is not so much like learning a list, but something much more dynamic, perhaps like learning to dance! The four-fold pattern of gathering, word, table, sending offers not only a framework for understanding the shape of eucharistic celebration, but also a sense of its rhythm and flow. It gives a sense of how holy communion shapes those who take part, drawing people together, inviting them to attend to God's story, nurturing their response, propelling them on with a purpose . . .

Exercise

Do you recognize this pattern from your own experience of worship?

The four-fold pattern clearly undergirds the materials developed in the Church of England's *Common Worship* resources. As the preface to *Common Worship* points out:

> The journey through the liturgy has a clear structure with signposts for those less familiar with the way. It moves from the gathering of the community through the Liturgy of the Word to an opportunity of transformation, sacramental or non-sacramental, after which those present are sent out to put their faith into practice.
>
> *Common Worship*, p. x

The same four-fold pattern can be found, as another example among many, clearly articulated in the *Methodist Worship Book* of 1999 which speaks of the 'fourfold structure of Preparation, Ministry of the Word, Response and Dismissal' (*Methodist Worship Book*, p. 26). There is also a clear sense that services of the word are intended to have not only a 'eucharistic shape', but that the 'response' section takes on a distinctly *eucharistic* accent. The book provides a range of *thanksgivings* for use in this part of its word-services.

Exercise

'Opportunity of transformation' is the powerful phrase that *Common Worship* uses to describe the third section of the four-fold structure of Christian worship. In what sense has the Eucharist ever seemed to offer this possibility to members of the group?

How might sacramental and non-sacramental worship at your church better allow for 'opportunities of transformation'?

Exercise

Use the orders for communion in *Common Worship* and trace the four-fold structure of gathering, word, table and sending. Could it be brought to greater clarity in your local orders of service?

The deep structure of the liturgy as 'gathering, word, table, sending' merits much attention, and for the rest of this section, we consider the headings in turn.

Gathering

In common with many other traditions, *Common Worship* uses 'The Gathering' as the heading for the opening section of the Eucharist. Whereas the last Church of England prayer book, the *Alternative Service*

Book (1980), used the title 'Preparation' for this part of the service, there is now the conscious use of a more theological word, for gathering is integral to the very meaning of 'liturgy', which is derived from the Greek words meaning 'people' and 'work': liturgy is, then, 'people's work', which requires that it is a communal enterprise, and never private, however personal. At a fundamental level, liturgy involves congregating, assembly.

Gathering to participate in the liturgy – A related point can be drawn from the fact that 'gathering' is itself a translation of the Greek work *synaxis*, which means 'come together'.[2] And following on from that, as the *Methodist Worship Book* puts it succinctly, 'the congregation is not an audience or a group of spectators' (*Methodist Worship Book* , p. vii). Liturgy is the people's work, and not simply that of the presiding minister. Hence, the great emphasis in so much of the literature on liturgical renewal on the notion of 'participation' as the basic and fundamental characteristic of liturgical celebration. The Roman Catholic Church's *Constitution on the Sacred Liturgy* gave this idea classic expression when it emphasized 'full, conscious and active participation' by all the people as 'demanded by the very nature of the liturgy' itself (*Constitution on the Sacred Liturgy*, p. 14). This bold statement is often considered to be 'an ecumenical treasure' across the Christian traditions, and sometimes regarded as the reason why the Second Vatican Council of the Roman Catholic Church has been regarded as the most significant thing to affect *Protestantism* in the twentieth century! As Gabe Huck elaborates on its meaning,

Why full and conscious and active participation? The answer is: That's liturgy. The answer is not: Because the Church has always taught this. The answer is not: Because the bishops say so. The answer is not: Because in some golden age of liturgy it was this way. None of this. Rather: Such participation – the full and active and conscious kind – is what we are after because that is 'the very nature of the liturgy'. In other words, no such participation, no liturgy . . . That means that it is the nature of

---

2 Although, rather confusingly, *synaxis* is often used in liturgical studies to refer to both the gathering and liturgy of the word.

the liturgy to be done by the people. It is not done to people. It is not done for people. It is not done in the presence of people. People do it and the plural is correct because it is as a Church assembled that people do liturgy.

Huck, 'The Very Nature of the Liturgy', p. 299

Participation, of course, has manifold expressions and involves things like quietude and silence as well as perhaps more obvious active modes. But participation is the basic purpose of gathering for liturgy.

Exercise

List ways in which it is possible to participate in liturgy. How many of these modes does worship at your church allow? How might the repertoire of participation be expanded?

However, the *challenge* of participation ought by no means to be underestimated in our cultural context, which is one that increasingly values individualism and the free exercise of personal choice.

The challenge of gathering – the challenge of gathering is particularly noted by some postmodern missiologists who speak of the 'problem' of liturgy in that gathering can so easily jar with cultural trends towards individualism. Some of them concede that churches must now dismantle 'congregational dynamics' if they are to better relate to society at large. Yet perhaps the very 'problem' of liturgy – its deeply communal nature – is in fact crucial to its missionary potential in contemporary culture? Gathering might in itself be seen as a counter-cultural activity, and gathering around the word and sacraments through which Christ Jesus is revealed might draw people out of their personal preferences and resist what Robert Bellah calls 'the narcissism of similarity'! Should it not be that the presence of Jesus Christ at the centre of the Church's gathering for worship nurtures a radical hospitality that stretches every tendency to individualism?

To concentrate on the face of Jesus Christ is to find our boundaries shifting and expanding as we slowly 'grasp what is the breadth and length and height and depth of Christ's love'. This is someone whose hospitality is universal – face by face by face. To be before his face is to find that he is looking with love on all sorts of unexpected, marginalized or to us disagreeable people, as well as on us. Wherever he is he brings them as part of his community. So we find our heart is overwhelmed in new ways by those to whom his gaze, words and actions direct us.

Ford, *The Shape of Living*, p. 22

As Gordon Lathrop asserts, to the gathering for worship Jesus 'brings with him all those who belong to him. That is a great crowd.' And, 'If it is truly Christ who comes, your heart will be filled with all the little and needy ones of the earth' (Lathrop, 'Liturgy and Mission', p. 202). Gathering for Christian worship is, therefore, an unambiguously *inclusive* activity. It throws out the challenge that to relate to God means engaging with others, inviting worshippers to make a modest enactment of the great commandments: '[Jesus said:] You shall love the Lord your God with all your heart, and with all your soul, and with all your mind. This is the greatest and first commandment. And a second is like it: You shall love your neighbour as yourself' (Matthew 22.37–40).

Word

The Eucharist is misunderstood if emphasis is placed exclusively on the table. The Emmaus encounter was one that involved the 'burning of hearts' as the scriptures were opened, as well as amazed recognition at the breaking of bread. Some Christian traditions now use as their primary title for the whole service of holy communion, 'A Service of Word and Table', making exactly the point that *word and sacrament belong together* (this title is used, for example, by the United Methodist Church of the United States). For some traditions, retaining or recovering a dual focus on word and table has meant that where they had perhaps historically emphasized one aspect – either word or sacrament – at the expense of the other, they have recently if not renamed, then redressed the balance of their celebrations. For example, it is obvious to note the ways in which the Roman Catholic tradition has in recent decades greatly heightened the role of scripture in celebration of the Mass. In the Roman context, the enlarged role of the scriptures in eucharistic celebration has been a response to the mandate of the Second Vatican Council that 'the treasures of the Bible are to be opened up more lavishly so that a richer fare may be provided for the faithful at the table of God's word' (*Constitution on the Sacred Liturgy*, p. 53). And one outcome of this mandate was a whole new lectionary provision for Roman Catholic worship, the *Lectionary for Mass* of 1981, which in turn formed the basis of the Revised Common Lectionary of 1992, which is now used (sometimes with slight adaptations, as in the Church of England) across increasing numbers of other churches. The lectionary means that shared attention to the same sections of scripture in turn Sunday by Sunday by countless Christians across the world has, alongside the common embrace of the four-fold pattern of eucharistic celebration, been the most significant expression of ecumenism in recent decades.

Table

Just as the renewal of Roman Catholic worship has involved enlarging the role of scripture in celebration, so more frequent sacramental celebration has, over recent decades, been a key to enriching worship in the Protestant churches. And such moves to make the Eucharist more central have in fact very often drawn contemporary Protestant traditions closer to the aspirations of the founders. Calvin and Cranmer, for instance, both hoped to encourage eucharistic celebration at least every Sunday. In Calvin's words, 'No assembly of the church should be held without the Word being preached, prayers being offered, and the Lord's Supper administered, and alms given' (*Institutes*, IV.xvii.44). The main activities of Sunday morning were, for Calvin, much as Justin broadly describes, and much as the World Council of Churches' 'Fundamental Ordo' is helping many Protestant traditions to recover.

Because aspects of sacramental spirituality will be the focus of our next chapter, at this point we can keep this section now brief before moving on to the last component of the four-fold structure, 'sending'. But before doing so, it is interesting to note just one or two ways in which attention to the early Church's understanding and practice of communion has provided some ways through Reformation and Counter-Reformation controversies. Many examples could of course be given, but one might be to note that recently it has become common for a range of Christian traditions to use both words 'table' and 'altar' to refer to the furniture necessary for holy communion. With Old Testament holy places like Bethel (Genesis 28.18–19) and Penuel (Genesis 32.30) as their inspiration, early Christians clearly used the term 'altar' to refer to the table around which the Eucharist was celebrated, and over time they tended to build altars in stone. However, at the Reformation – for a range of reasons – the term 'altar' fell out of use among Protestants, stone altars were often removed from church buildings and replaced by wooden tables. A reference to 'the altar' on page 46 of *New Patterns for Worship* (2002) is the first use of this term in an official prayer book of the Church of England since 1549!

The early Church also provides inspiration for recovery of gestures for worship, as well as words for it. A remarkable study called *The Postures of the Assembly During the Eucharistic Prayer* (Leonard and Mitchell, 1994) reveals that for many centuries, in at least some places, the whole people of God raised their hands for the eucharistic prayer in the posture often now retained by the priest at the altar. Early Christians understood this as a sign of thanksgiving – a *gesture* of 'eucharist' – but also as more: stretching out the arms shapes the body into a shape of the cross, it says 'sacrifice'. This posture, recovered from the early Church as a posture for *all God's people*, rather than priest alone, has recently found some strong advocates (e.g. Giles, *Creating Uncommon Worship*, pp. 163–4).

Exercise

Consider your experience of the eucharistic prayer: does it feel like a central feature of the liturgy? Should celebration of eucharistic prayer be enlivened, and how could this happen?

Sending

One of the important gifts of Reformed churches to contemporary ecumenical embrace of the four-fold deep structure of the Eucharist has been to emphasize the fourth section: 'sending'. Recently, some Reformed traditions have placed a 'word of mission' at the turning from table into sending. For example, in *Uniting in Worship* of the Uniting Church of Australia (comprised of former Presbyterian and Methodist people), verses from scripture are suggested for proclamation as means of orienting worshippers on their calling to go and share God's mission in the world. Some of the suggested scriptures include: Deuteronomy 31.6; Micah 6.8; Matthew 5.14, 16; Matthew 28.19–20; Acts 1.8; Romans 12.1; 1 Corinthians 16.13, 14; 2 Corinthians 5.18, 20; Colossians 3.17; 1 Peter 2.21; 4.13; and 1 John 3.23.

Exercise

Look up some of these scripture readings. How do they speak of the mission of the Christian people?

Many Anglicans may remember the use of pithy, though variable, scripture readings at this point in the orders of holy communion in the *Alternative Service Book* of 1980. This was an echo of the Reformed tradition of placing a 'word of mission' at this moment.[3] The *Common Worship* orders tend not to use sentences from scripture at this point, although the language of prayer in the 'sending' part of the the service is strongly oriented to turning in witness and service to the world God loves: they 'offer' God 'our souls and bodies' to be a 'living sacrifice', an echo of Romans 12.1. They ask to be 'sent out in the power of [the] Spirit', to live the risen life of Christ, to bring life, to give light, to others (*Common Worship*, p. 182). Similarly, a daring prayer from the contemporary liturgical resources

---

3 The Roman Catholic Mass, prior to Vatican II, also included a 'last Gospel' at this point in the order, although its purpose was somewhat different.

of the Episcopal Church in the USA asks God to send out the people as 'a people forgiven, healed, renewed' to proclaim God's love and live the risen life of Christ (*Enriching Our Worship*, p. 70).

The Orthodox sometimes call this sending out 'the liturgy after the liturgy', and the new Baptist prayer book uses a liturgical text that underlines the point of sending: its dismissal reads, 'Our worship is ended', to which the people respond, 'Our service begins' (*Gathering for Worship*, p. 21).

In these various ways, the final part of the four-fold deep structure of the Eucharist involves a vigorous turn to the world, and it is one that is oriented to mission. By drawing the world to worshippers' attention, eucharistic celebration might be said to be 'mission-shaped', to use a phrase that is much in vogue in the Church of England at the moment (*Mission-Shaped Church*, 2004). Or to employ an alternative term that is favoured by the Evangelical Lutheran Church in the United States, eucharistic celebration turns assemblies 'inside out' (Shattauer, *Inside Out*).

Exercise

The idea of a 'mission-shaped church' is much discussed at the moment. Can you imagine the four-fold celebration as 'mission-shaped worship'? For instance, how does it turn worshippers towards the world to share in God's purposes? Discuss any lived experience of this dynamic and how your congregation might become excited about it.

Exercise

Imagine a four-week sermon series that covers in turn the blessings and challenges of gathering, word, table and sending. What are some of the key things you might want to say about each of these eucharistic themes?

3

Eucharistic Spirituality: 'Living the Thanksgiving'

Senses of the body

Finally, we turn to consider some aspects of eucharistic spirituality. Having in earlier chapters considered mainly *texts* from biblical, early Christian and contemporary sources, this chapter invites us to reflect upon the ritual *gestures* involved in holy communion that communicate a sense of 'the body of Christ'.

The liturgy document of the Second Vatican Council (*Constitution on the Sacred Liturgy*) affirmed what is sometimes said to be a 'dispersed' presence of Christ in the Eucharist. It located Christ's presence in the minister, in the bread and wine (which it refers to as the 'eucharistic species'), in sacramental action, in the word, and in the worshipping people:

Christ is always present in His Church, especially in her liturgical celebrations. He is present in the sacrifice of the Mass, not only in the person of His minister, 'the same now offering, through the ministry of priests, who formerly offered himself on the cross' (20), but especially under the eucharistic species. By His power He is present in the sacraments, so that when a man baptizes it is really Christ Himself who baptizes (21). He is present in His word, since it is He Himself who speaks when the holy scriptures are read in the Church. He is present, lastly, when the Church prays and sings, for He promised: 'Where two or three are gathered together in my name, there am I in the midst of them' (Matthew 18.20).   *Constitution on the Sacred Liturgy*, p. 7

While retaining some traditional Catholic emphases (such as suggesting that divine presence is 'especially' identified with the bread and wine), and while some Protestants might still want to nuance the statement to better suit their tastes, as it stands it can nevertheless be seen as deeply hospitable to ecumenical understanding. Its affirmation of 'dispersed' divine presence at the Eucharist is in line with the shift, across the Christian traditions, away from limited 'localization' of the presence of Christ: divine self-giving is to be found not only in the elements of bread and wine, but poured out upon the word, action, people, and minister.

Exercise

Observe the way in which the ceremonial of holy communion in your parish either 'disperses' or 'localizes' the sense of the body of Christ. What does the ceremonial suggest and how might the ceremonial be adapted to better allow for a contemporary dispersed sense of presence?

Consider next, then, the Roman Catholic liturgical theologian Michael Joncas' reflections on how to pay heed to the ambiguous overlapping of 'the presence of Christ' *in the action of sharing* the sacrament. Joncas is conscious both of the possibilities of thoughtlessly or unintentionally limiting the sense of divine presence and also of how alliances of words and gestures can facilitate a lively sacramental spirituality. This extract from his writing on 'ritual transformations' raises fascinating questions about how such insights might be appropriated in other traditions too:

There's a catch phrase in counselling psychology. 'What you are doing speaks so loudly that I can't hear what you're saying.' . . .'

[Consider the practice of receiving] Holy Communion. The minister of Communion extends the consecrated host or broken bread towards the recipient and declares, 'The body of Christ'. I suspect that if we were to poll most recipients and ask 'What does this mean?' they would say, in these or other words, 'The gesture enshrines a declarative understanding of the text: This is the body of Christ'. This interpretation of the gesture and its statement is so widespread that . . . a fair number of eucharistic ministers have taken it on themselves to add those words to the text: 'Oh, Heather, this is the body of Christ'. (Of course I'm going to bracket here the discussion of this metaphoric interchange, since the one thing that should be obvious to both the minister and recipient is that the consecrated host is not the body of Christ in exactly the same way as blood, bones, and organs were the body of the historical Jesus.) There is a wisdom, however, in the ritual's refusal to make this text a declarative statement, because then the gesture may modify the denotation carried by the text with rich, symbolic connotation. The 'body' announced by the text may have as its first referent the consecrated host, but it also carries the connotations of the minister's providing and the recipient's receiving, the common eating and drinking, the processional activity of those coming to and moving away from the common eating and drinking. All of these are the body of Christ. These connotations depend on how the minister and recipient make eye contact, what tone of voice the minister uses, how the recipient articulates 'Amen', and whether or not the host is placed on the hand or the tongue.

Joncas, 'Ritual Transformations', pp. 51–2

Exercise

Having read this extract, consider your experience of sharing the sacramental elements of holy communion, and think about how meanings of 'the body of Christ' converge.

A spirituality of the Eucharist is likely to best flourish in the kind of environment where the *liturgical action* affirms the 'dispersed' presence of Christ, and in which the ceremonial serves to help the congregation's understanding that they *themselves* might be sacramental, that they must become the body of Christ. As Augustine preached to the people gathered for communion: 'be what you see, become what you are'.

The modern theologian Don Saliers affirms Augustine's ancient call. He writes of the purpose of the Christian people being to embody the eucharistic action of 'taking, blessing, breaking and giving' (e.g. Mark 14.22; Luke 22.19) bread and wine. The action in which the Church both remembers and joins Jesus in eucharistic celebration is itself a pattern for Christian spirituality, and *we encounter grace in living in the way the celebration unfolds*:

- Just as bread and wine are *taken* we are to offer ourselves into God's hands, to give ourselves to God's purposes.
- Just as thanksgiving is raised up, we are to 'live the thanksgiving', in gratitude for the mighty acts of God that the eucharistic prayer narrates, 'leaning into' its proclamation.
- Just as bread is broken and wine poured out, we must be vulnerable to all faith demands.
- Just as nourishment is shared, so we 'must be prepared to be given for others' (Saliers, *Worship and Spirituality*, pp. 67–8).

This is the heart of the dynamic of the Eucharist: 'Grace is given in the eucharist, but this is the grace we also encounter in offering, blessing, breaking open, and sharing our lives with all in this needy world' (Saliers, *Worship and Spirituality*, p. 68).

Exercise

Consider the liturgical action around the holy table – taking, blessing, breaking, giving – as a pattern of life. How might it be mapped onto your own aspirations for life in the Spirit? And how might it shape a sense of congregational mission?

References and Further Reading

References in text

Bruce Chilton, 1997, *Jesus' Prayer and Jesus' Eucharist: His Personal Practice of Spirituality*, Valley Forge, PA: Trinity Press International

Common Worship: Services and Prayers for the Church of England, 2000, London: Church House Publishing

Constitution on the Sacred Liturgy, 1975, Austin Flannery, ed., *Vatican II: Conciliar and Post-Conciliar Documents*, New York: Costello

Enriching Our Worship: Supplemental Liturgical Resources, Volume 1, 1997, New York: Church Publishing

David F. Ford, 1997, *The Shape of Living*, London: Fount

Gathering for Worship: Patterns and Prayers for the Community of Disciples by the Baptist Union of Great Britain, 2005, Norwich: Canterbury Press

Richard Giles, 2004, *Creating Uncommon Worship: Transforming the Liturgy of the Eucharist*, Norwich: Canterbury Press

Robert Hovda, 1990, 'Liturgy Shaping Us in the Christian Life', in Eleanor Bernstein, ed., *Liturgy and Spirituality in Context: Perspectives on Prayer and Culture*, Collegeville, MN: Liturgical Press, pp. 136–50

Gabe Huck, ed., 1994, *A Sourcebook about Liturgy*, Chicago, IL: Liturgy Training Publications

Gabe Huck, 1998, 'The Very Nature of the Liturgy', in Kathleen Hughes, ed., *Finding Voice to Give God Praise: Essays in the Many Languages of Liturgy*, Collegeville, MN: Liturgical Press, pp. 299–309

R. C. D. Jasper and Geoffrey Cuming, eds, 1987, *Prayers of the Eucharist: Early and Reformed*, 3rd edn, Collegeville, MN: Liturgical Press

Michael Joncas, 2003, 'Ritual Transformations: Principles, Patterns, and Peoples', in Gabe Huck, ed., *Toward Ritual Transformation: Remembering Robert Hovda*, Collegeville, MN: Liturgical Press, pp. 49–69

Gordon W. Lathrop, 1993, *Holy Things: A Liturgical Theology*, Minneapolis, MN: Fortress Press

Gordon W. Lathrop, 1999, 'Liturgy and Mission in the North American Context', in Thomas Schattauer, ed., *Inside Out: Worship in an Age of Mission*, Minneapolis, MN: Fortress Press, pp. 201–12

John K. Leonard and Nathan D. Mitchell, 1994, *The Postures of the Assembly During the Eucharistic Prayer*, Chicago, IL: Liturgy Training Publications

The Methodist Worship Book, 1999, Peterborough: Methodist Publishing House

Mission-Shaped Church: Church Planting and Fresh Expressions of Church in a Changing Context, 2004, London: Church House Publishing

Don E. Saliers, 1996, *Worship and Spirituality*, 2nd edn, Akron, OH: Order of St Luke

Thomas Schattauer, ed., 1999, *Inside Out: Worship in an Age of Mission*, Minneapolis, MN: Fortress Press

Further reading

Thomas Best and Dagmar Heller, eds, 1995, *Eucharistic Worship in Ecumenical Contexts: The Lima Liturgy and Beyond*, Geneva: World Council of Churches

Paul Bradshaw, 2004, *Eucharistic Origins*, London: SPCK

Bruce Chilton, 1997, *Jesus' Prayer and Jesus' Eucharist: His Personal Practice of Spirituality*, Valley Forge, PA: Trinity Press International

Edward Foley, 1990, *From Age to Age: How Christians Have Celebrated the Eucharist*, Chicago: Liturgy Training Publications

Richard Giles, 2004, *Creating Uncommon Worship: Transforming the Liturgy of the Eucharist*, Norwich: Canterbury Press

David Holeton, ed., 1998, *Our Thanks and Praise: The Eucharist in Anglicanism Today*, Toronto: Anglican Book Centre

Gordon W. Lathrop, 1993, *Holy Things: A Liturgical Theology*, Minneapolis, MN: Fortress Press

Gail Ramshaw, 1994, *Words Around the Table*, Chicago, IL: Liturgy Training Publications

Don E. Saliers, 1996, *Worship and Spirituality*, 2nd edn, Akron, OH: Order of St Luke

David Stancliffe, 2003, *God's Pattern: Shaping our Worship, Ministry and Life*, London: SPCK

Laurence Hull Stookey, 1993, *Eucharist: Christ's Feast with the Church*, Nashville, TN: Abingdon Press